STECK-VAUGHN

Vocabulary Advantage FOR American History

Vocabulary Journal

Steck Vaughn

A Harcourt Achieve Imprint

www.Steck-Vaughn.com

1-800-531-5015

Acknowledgements

Executive Editor Eduardo Aparicio
Senior Editor Victoria Davis
Design Team Cynthia Ellis, Cynthia Hannon, Jean O'Dette
Media Researchers Nicole Mlakar, Stephanie Arsenault
Production Team Mychael Ferris-Pacheco, Paula Schumann, Alia Hasan
Creative Team Joan Cunningham, Alan Klemp
Illustrations Missi Jay

Photo Credits
Page 19e ©William Whitehurst/CORBIS; p. 20 and 21 ©Bettmann/CORBIS; p. 23e ©The Granger Collection; p. 29e ©CORBIS; p. 33e and 35 ©Bettmann/CORBIS; p. 36 ©CORBIS; p. 47c and 54 ©Swim Ink 2, LLC/CORBIS; p. 57c ©Najlah Feanny/ CORBIS SABA; p. 61 ©The Granger Collection; p. 63 ©Bettmann/CORBIS; p. 65e ©The Granger Collection; p. 67 and 71 ©Bettmann/ CORBIS; p. 73 ©The Granger Collection; p. 74 ©Neville Elder/CORBIS; p. 77c ©Michael Rougier/Time Life Pictures/Getty Images.

Additional photography by Comstock Royalty Free, Corel Royalty Free, FDR Library, Getty Images Royalty Free, LBJ Library, Minnesota Historical Society, Park Street Photography, Photos.com Royalty Free, Royalty-Free/CORBIS, and Stockbyte Royalty Free.

Harcourt Achieve

ISBN 1-4190-1930-9

Printed in the United States of America
2 3 4 5 6 7 8 032 12 11 10 09 08 07

Table of Contents

How to Use This Journal

This journal is for you! You can use it to create your own understanding of new words. You can also use it to keep track of these words.

Step 1: Find your New American History Words in the journal.
Step 2: Write a definition for each word.
Step 3: Answer the question with a full sentence.
Step 4: Write
- **synonyms** or **antonyms** of the new word.
- a word or words **related** to the new word.
- the **root, prefix,** or **suffix** of the new word and its **meaning**.
- **other meanings** and **parts of speech** of the new word.
- an **example** or **description** of the new word.
- **clue words** that help you remember what the new word means.

Step 5: Create your own definitions for the Other Useful Words.

You can also add any other new words you want to remember. And, there's space for you to draw pictures. Drawing a picture can sometimes help you remember a new word.

Enjoy your journal!

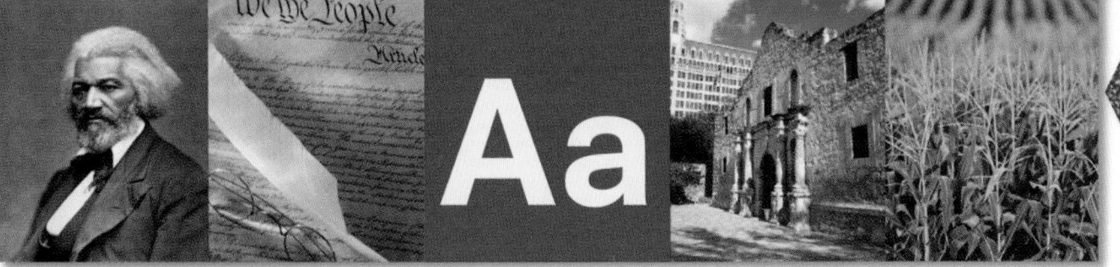

abolition (n.)________________________________

____

____

What verb is the word **abolition** related to?____________

____

____

____

Synonym________________________________

____

Frederick Douglass

agriculture (n.)________________________________

____

____

What are some products of **agriculture**?____________

____

____

____

Root word and meaning________________________

____

Aa

ally (n.)____

____

____

Who is your greatest **ally**?_____________________________

____

____

____

Antonym____

____

amendment (n.)____

____

____

Why might someone make an **amendment**?__________________

____

____

____

Clue words____

____

Aa

amnesty (n.)________________________________

____

____

When have you been shown **amnesty**?______________

____

____

____

Synonyms________________________________

____

appeasement (n.)____________________________

____

____

Describe an act of **appeasment** you have seen or performed.________________________________

____

____

Root word and meaning__________________________

____

apprentice (n.)________________________________

____

____

Who would you like to be an **apprentice** to? Why?_____

____

____

____

Other meanings and parts of speech________________

____

armistice (n.)_________________________________

____

____

What are the benefits of an **armistice**?______________

____

____

____

Root word and meaning__________________________

____

Aa

artifact (n.)

What can you learn from an **artifact**?

Example

assembly (n.)

Have you ever been a part of an **assembly**? Describe.

Other meanings and parts of speech

Aa

agriculture

border (n.)______________________________

What countries share **borders** with the United States?

Other meanings and parts of speech____________________

boycott (v.)______________________________

What might make you **boycott** a business?________________

Other meanings and parts of speech____________________

Bb

Draw it!

Aa Bb **Cc** Dd Ee Ff Gg Hh Ii Jj Kk Ll Mm Nn Oo Pp Qq Rr Ss Tt Uu Vv Ww Xx Yy Zz

canal (n.)____

What can a **canal** be used for?________________________

Examples____

capital (n.)____

What do you need **capital** for?________________________

Other meanings and parts of speech________________________

Cc

capitalism (n.)________________________________

____

____

What are some features of **capitalism**?______________

____

____

____

Suffix and meaning______________________________

____

charter (n.)__________________________________

____

____

What is the purpose of a **charter**?_________________

____

____

____

Other meanings and parts of speech_______________

____

Cc

civilization (n.)

What would be in your perfect **civilization**?

Suffix and meaning

colony (n.)

Name a country that built a **colony** in North America.

Related words

Aa Bb Cc Dd Ee Ff Gg Hh Ii Jj Kk Ll Mm Nn Oo Pp Qq Rr Ss Tt Uu Vv Ww Xx Yy Zz

Cc

communism (n.)______________________________

____

____

How is **communism** different from capitalism?________

____

____

____

Root word and meaning__________________________

____

compromise (v.)______________________________

____

____

Describe a time you have had to **compromise** with someone.___________________________________

____

____

Other meanings and parts of speech________________

____

Cc

confederacy (n.)

What are some features of a **confederacy**?

Related words

congress (n.)

What does a **congress** do?

Synonym

Cc

conservation (n.)______________________________

Why is **conservation** important?____________________

Root word and meaning________________________

containment (n.)______________________________

What is the purpose of **containment**?________________

Root word and meaning________________________

Cc

convert (v.)______________________________

How could you **convert** someone to be a fan of your favorite sport team?________________

Other meanings and parts of speech____________

corporation (n.)________________________

Would you choose to work for a **corporation**? Why?

Examples______________________________

Cc

covenant (n.)______________________________

Why might people make **covenants**?__________________

Clue words________________________________

culture (n.)_______________________________

What things do many **cultures** have in common?________

Related words_____________________________

Cc

Cc

canal

deficit (n.)____

____

____

How does a **deficit** happen?________________________

____

____

____

Antonym____

____

democracy (n.)___________________________________

____

____

What makes a **democracy** different from other kinds of government?____________________________________

____

____

Related words______________________________________

____

Dd

depression (n.)____________________

What can cause a **depression**?__________

Other meanings and parts of speech__________

disarmament (n.)____________________

What happens during a **disarmament**?__________

Related words____________________

Dd

discrimination (n.)______________________________

____

____

What kinds of **discrimination** are there?_____________

____

____

____

Prefix and meaning______________________________

____

dissenter (n.)__________________________________

____

____

What things might a **dissenter** do?_________________

____

____

____

Root word and meaning___________________________

____

Dd

domesticate (v.)____

What animals have been **domesticated** by humans?____

Root word and meaning________________________________

duties (n.)____

What are some of your daily **duties**?_________________

Synonyms____

emancipation (n.)____

What are some kinds of **emancipation**?______________________________________

Describe____

empire (n.)____

What are some **empires** you've learned about?______________________________

Related words____

Ee

enterprise (n.)____

What **enterprise** would you like to take on?________________

Synonym____

entrepreneur (n.) ____________________________________

If you were an **entrepreneur**, what kind of business would you have?____________________________________

Examples____

Ee

environment (n.)____

Describe the **environment** in which you live.

Suffix and meaning

escalation (n.)

How can you stop the **escalation** of an argument?

Describe

Aa Bb Cc Dd **Ee** Ff Gg Hh Ii Jj Kk Ll Mm Nn Oo Pp Qq Rr Ss Tt Uu Vv Ww Xx Yy Zz

Ee

exchange (v.)____

What is something you have **exchanged** with a friend?

Prefix and meaning__________________________________

executive (adj.)_____________________________________

What should someone in an **executive** job be good at?

Other meanings and parts of speech____________________

Ee

expatriate (n.)

Why might someone become an **expatriate**?

Describe

expedition (n.)

Where would you like to go on an **expedition**?

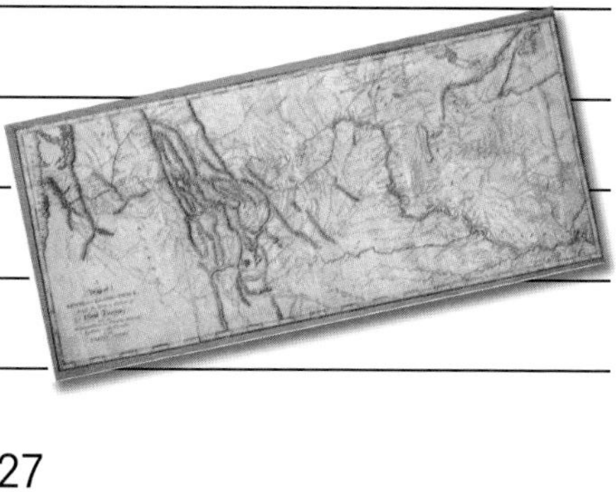

Clue words

Aa Bb Cc Dd **Ee** Ff Gg Hh Ii Jj Kk Ll Mm Nn Oo Pp Qq Rr Ss Tt Uu Vv Ww Xx Yy Zz

Ee

export (v.)____________________

What are some things that can be **exported**?__________

Other meanings and parts of speech__________

Aa Bb Cc Dd Ee Ff Gg Hh Ii Jj Kk Ll Mm Nn Oo Pp Qq Rr Ss Tt Uu Vv Ww Xx Yy Zz

fascism (n.)______________________________

____

____

What are some features of **fascism**?____________

____

____

____

Clue words________________________________

____

federalism (n.)____________________________

____

____

What are some things that states control under **federalism**?____________________________

____

____

Suffix and meaning__________________________

____

Ff

frontier (n.)____

What do you think the **frontier** was like?________________

Clue words____

Aa Bb Cc Dd Ee Ff **Gg** **Hh** Ii Jj Kk Ll Mm Nn Oo Pp Qq Rr Ss Tt Uu Vv Ww Xx Yy Zz

genocide (n.)____________________

What makes people commit **genocide**?____________________

Root word and meaning____________________

Gg Hh

highway

Aa Bb Cc Dd Ee Ff Gg Hh Ii Jj Kk Ll Mm Nn Oo Pp Qq Rr Ss Tt Uu Vv Ww Xx Yy Zz

immigration (n.)______________________________

____

____

How does **immigration** change a country?______________________________

____

____

____

Prefix and meaning______________________________

____

imperialism (n.)______________________________

____

____

How does **imperialism** change a country?______________________________

____

____

____

Related words______________________________

____

import (v.)______________________________________

____

____

Why would a country **import** certain things?__________

____

____

____

Root word and meaning______________________________

____

indentured (adj.)__________________________________

____

____

What was life like for an **indentured** servant?_________

____

____

____

Clue words_____________________________________

____

independence (n.)____________________

How do you show your **independence**?__________

Root word and meaning____________________

integration (n.)____________________

What things can be **integrated**?__________

Synonyms____________________

Ii

interchangeable (adj.)________________________

What are some things that are **interchangeable**?______

Prefix and meaning________________________

internment (n.)________________________

What happens to people during **internment**?__________

Root word and meaning________________________

intolerance (n.)

How can you change people's **intolerance** of others?

Antonyms

isolationism (n.)

Why might a country have a policy of **isolationism**?

Root word and meaning

Ii

independence

judicial (adj.)

What does someone in a **judicial** job do?

Root word and meaning

Jj Kk

Draw it!

legislate (v.)____

____

____

If you were a leader, what would you **legislate**?__________

____

____

____

Related words____

____

liberate (v.)____

____

____

How might you **liberate** someone from a bad situation?

____

____

Related words____

____

____

manufacturing (n.)____________________

List one good and one bad thing about **manufacturing**.

Root word and meaning____________________

mercantilism (n.)____________________

What are some features of **mercantilism**?____________________

Clue words____________________

Mm

mercenary (n.)______________________________

____

____

What are some differences between a **mercenary** and a regular soldier?______________________________

____

____

Suffix and meaning____________________________

____

migration (n.)______________________________

____

____

What makes people and animals choose **migration** over staying someplace?______________________________

____

____

Related words______________________________

____

Mm

Aa Bb Cc Dd Ee Ff Gg Hh Ii Jj Kk Ll **Mm** Nn Oo Pp Qq Rr Ss Tt Uu Vv Ww Xx Yy Zz

militarism (n.)______________________________

What are some features of **militarism**?__________________

Root word and meaning____________________

militia (n.)______________________________

Why might someone join a **militia**?__________________

Related words______________________________

Mm

missionary (n.)________________________________

____

____

What kind of work does a **missionary** do?____________

____

____

____

Root word and meaning________________________

____

mobilize (v.)________________________________

____

____

What might you **mobilize** your friends to do?_________

____

____

____

Suffix and meaning___________________________

____

nationalism (n.)____________________________________

How do Americans show their **nationalism**?____________

Synonym____

nativist (n.)_______________________________________

What things might a **nativist** support?_______________

Suffix and meaning__________________________________

Nn Oo

neutral (adj.)______________________________

What are some things you are **neutral** about?__________

Antonyms______________________________

nuclear (adj.)______________________________

What are some things that can be described as **nuclear**?

Related words______________________________

Nn Oo

Aa
Bb
Cc
Dd
Ee
Ff
Gg
Hh
Ii
Jj
Kk
Ll
Mm
Nn
Oo
Pp
Qq
Rr
Ss
Tt
Uu
Vv
Ww
Xx
Yy
Zz

Draw it!

Nn Oo

Draw it!

Aa Bb Cc Dd Ee Ff Gg Hh Ii Jj Kk Ll Mm Nn Oo Pp Qq Rr Ss Tt Uu Vv Ww Xx Yy Zz

patriot (n.)__________

What are some things that a **patriot** might do?__________

Related words__________

petition (n.)__________

What might you write a **petition** for?__________

Other meanings and parts of speech__________

Pp

pilgrim (n.)

What might be a **pilgrim's** goals?

Describe

pioneer (n.)

Who is a modern **pioneer**?

Other meanings and parts of speech

Pp

plantation (n.)____

____

____

What kind of work happened on a **plantation**?__________

____

____

____

Describe____

____

progressive (n.)______________________________________

____

____

What things might a **progressive** try to change?________

____

____

____

Root word and meaning______________________________

____

Pp

prohibition (n.)________________________________

What are some **prohibitions** you follow at school?

Root word and meaning________________________

propaganda (n.)________________________________

How might you know if something is **propaganda**?

Examples________________________________

Pp

proprietor (n.)______________________________

Who is the **proprietor** of your favorite store?__________

Synonyms______________________________

Pp

pueblo

Woof

quota (n.)____

How can you make sure you reach your **quota** of sleep each night?__________________________________

Clue words____

Qq

quilt

range (n.)

Where might you find a **range**?

Other meanings and parts of speech

rebellion (n.)

Why might someone start a **rebellion**?

Root word and meaning

Aa Bb Cc Dd Ee Ff Gg Hh Ii Jj Kk Ll Mm Nn Oo Pp Qq **Rr** Ss Tt Uu Vv Ww Xx Yy Zz

Rr

reconstruction (n.)____________________________________

____

____

What happened during **reconstruction**?________________

____

____

____

Prefix and meaning_____________________________________

____

region (n.)____

____

____

What **region** of the country do you live in?______________

____

____

____

Synonyms____

____

Rr

relief (n.)

What organizations provide **relief** to people who have suffered?

Other meanings and parts of speech

removal (n.)

Why were certain groups chosen for **removal** from the land?

Other meanings and parts of speech

Aa Bb Cc Dd Ee Ff Gg Hh Ii Jj Kk Ll Mm Nn Oo Pp Qq **Rr** Ss Tt Uu Vv Ww Xx Yy Zz

Rr

reparations (n.)____________________________________

____

____

What might a group receive **reparations** for?__________

____

____

____

Synonyms____

____

repeal (v.)____

____

____

What things might people ask leaders to **repeal**?________

____

____

____

Antonyms____

____

Rr

representative (n.)______________________________

Who would you like to be your **representative** to talk with your principal? Why?____________________

Root word and meanings____________________

republic (n.)______________________________

What are some features of a **republic**?____________________

Related words______________________________

Aa Bb Cc Dd Ee Ff Gg Hh Ii Jj Kk Ll Mm Nn Oo Pp Qq **Rr** Ss Tt Uu Vv Ww Xx Yy Zz

Rr

retaliation (n.)______________________________

What are some kinds of **retaliation**?________________

Synonyms______________________________

revolution (n.)______________________________

What are some possible results of a **revolution**?________

Related words______________________________

sanctions (n.)____________________

How might **sanctions** harm a country?__________

Clue words____________________

secede (v.)____________________

Why might a state want to **secede**?__________

Related words____________________

UNION

SECESSIONISTS LEAVING THE UNION

Ss

sect (n.)____________________________

What might make people want to form a **sect**?__________

Synonyms____________________________

sedition (n.)____________________________

Why might someone commit **sedition**?__________

Examples____________________________

Ss

segregation (n.)

What are some examples of **segregation**?

Antonyms

self-determination (n.)

Why might smaller countries want **self-determination**?

Related words

Ss

settlement (n.)____

What would it have been like to live in an early American **settlement**?____

Root word and meaning____________________

slavery (n.)____

How did **slavery** end in the United States?____________________

Related words____

Ss

socialism (n.)____________________________________

____

____

What makes **socialism** different from capitalism?______

____

____

____

Root word and meaning____________________________

____

society (n.)____________________________________

____

____

What are some rules you have to follow in American **society**?__________________________________

____

____

Describe____

____

Ss

sovereignty (n.)____

Why would a country want **sovereignty**?______________

Clue words____

staple (adj.)____

What is a **staple** food in your home?______________

Other meanings and parts of speech______________

Ss

suffrage (n.)

Why is it important for everyone to have **suffrage**?

NEW YORK CITY WOMEN HAVE NO VOTE AT ALL.

Clue words

Aa Bb Cc Dd Ee Ff Gg Hh Ii Jj Kk Ll Mm Nn Oo Pp Qq Rr Ss Tt Uu Vv Ww Xx Yy Zz

Ss

tariff (n.)

When might a **tariff** be unfair?

Synonyms

territory (n.)

What places do you consider your **territory**?

Synonyms

Aa Bb Cc Dd Ee Ff Gg Hh Ii Jj Kk Ll Mm Nn Oo Pp Qq Rr Ss Tt Uu Vv Ww Xx Yy Zz

Tt Uu

terrorism (n.)____

What are some of the effects of **terrorism**?____________

Root word and meaning_________________________________

textile (n.)____

What things are made out of **textiles**?________________

Synonyms____

Tt Uu

totalitarianism (n.)________________________________

What power does a common citizen have under **totalitarianism**? Why?____________________

Describe______________________________________

treaty (n.)____________________________________

What information might be in a **treaty**?____________________

Examples______________________________________

Tt Uu

trust (n.)____

How are **trusts** bad for an economy?__________________

Other meanings and parts of speech__________________

welfare (n.)

How does **welfare** help people?

Other meanings and parts of speech

Aa Bb Cc Dd Ee Ff Gg Hh Ii Jj Kk Ll Mm Nn Oo Pp Qq Rr Ss Tt Uu Vv Ww Xx Yy Zz

Vv Ww

the West

XxYyZz

Aa
Bb
Cc
Dd
Ee
Ff
Gg
Hh
Ii
Jj
Kk
Ll
Mm
Nn
Oo
Pp
Qq
Rr
Ss
Tt
Uu
Vv
Ww
Xx
Yy
Zz
Draw it!

XxYyZz

Draw it!

Other Useful Words

abbreviate____

analyze____

assume____

conclude____

confirm____

contrast____

debate____

define____

describe____

emphasize____

expand____

____

factor____

____

highlight______________________________________

____

illustrate______________________________________

____

indicate_______________________________________

____

inform____

____

objective______________________________________

____

omit____

____

organize_______________________________________

____

portray____

____

predict ____

____

propose ____

____

relate ____

____

respond ____

____

review ____

____

sequence ____

____

specify ____

____

speculate ____

____

summarize ____

____

survey ____

____

What's That?

Have you been wondering what's in those pictures at the top of each letter's first page? Here's a list! Look at the pictures again and discuss these questions with a partner:

- How are these things connected to the American History words I've learned?
- What other names could you give these pictures?

Aa	abolitionist, amendment, the Alamo, agriculture
Bb	barbed wire, ballot box, buffalo, bridge
Cc	conservation, culture, Confederacy, compass
Dd	desert, dollar, debt, drilling
Ee	emission, economy, expedition, export
Ff	frontier, farmer, fighter plane, factory
Gg Hh	Grand Canyon, highway
Ii	Iwo Jima monument, Independence Day, import, iron
Jj Kk	justice, kachina doll
Ll	legislation, Statue of Liberty, livestock, labor
Mm	manufacturing, migrate, militarism, mission
Nn Oo	Native American, Oregon Trail
Pp	patriot, pioneer, prospector, pueblo
Qq	quarter, quilt
Rr	railroad, resource, revolution, range
Ss	silver, strike, space shuttle, social security
Tu Uu	television, urban
Vv Ww	volcano, the West
Xx Yy Zz	Yalta Conference, Zapotec carving